One Last Souvenir

Naomi Church

theophilus press
Oneonta, New York

The body text of this volume is printed in 11.5 pt Times Roman
and the poem titles are printed in 22 pt. Zapf Chancery.
Varied settings are incidental.

ISBN 1-881579-05-0
Registered with the
United States Library of Congress

theophilus press
HC 64 Box 40
Rt. 28/Franklin Mt.
Oneonta, NY 13820

Church, Naomi, *One Last Souvenir*
(Oneonta, NY: theophilus press, 1993), 80pp.

For my husband:

Glenn

"True ease in writing comes from art, not chance,
As those move easiest who have learned to dance."
Alexander Pope

Table of Contents

Foreword

There have been three consecutive generations of poets in our family, beginning with the oldest, me. Next came our late son, William S. Church, author of *Windingsheets of Vineleaf*, currently used to teach poetry in several school systems.

The third generation produced three more: Bill's daughter, Leslie Anne Church, and our grandson, William Glenn Howells are both carrying on the family tradition of writing poetry. The latest addition is our six-year old grand-daughter, Krista Lynn Church, who recently received recognition in a grade school poetry competition.

As for acknowledgements: To God, Who makes all things possible; to Glenn, my husband for 56 years, who patiently helped me with every phase and made this book a reality; our daughter, Betsy Howells, for typing and proofreading the manuscript; Margaret Howells, who helped with the editing; my sister, Ruth Brenner, for a generous financial contribution toward publishing costs; Anne Church, our daughter-in-law, for advice and sharing her own publishing experience; Jeffrey Paterson, a talented writer friend who did the summary on the back cover; Dottie Farrell, a local artist and calligrapher who created the fine book cover I had envisioned; Parke Morrow, Jr., of The Book Corner; Monica Toohey Haack, a Minnesota poet; and poet Margaret A. Robbins, all of whom came up with fine ideas and suggestions; and to everyone who assisted in any way at the birth of my "baby." My sincere thanks to you all!

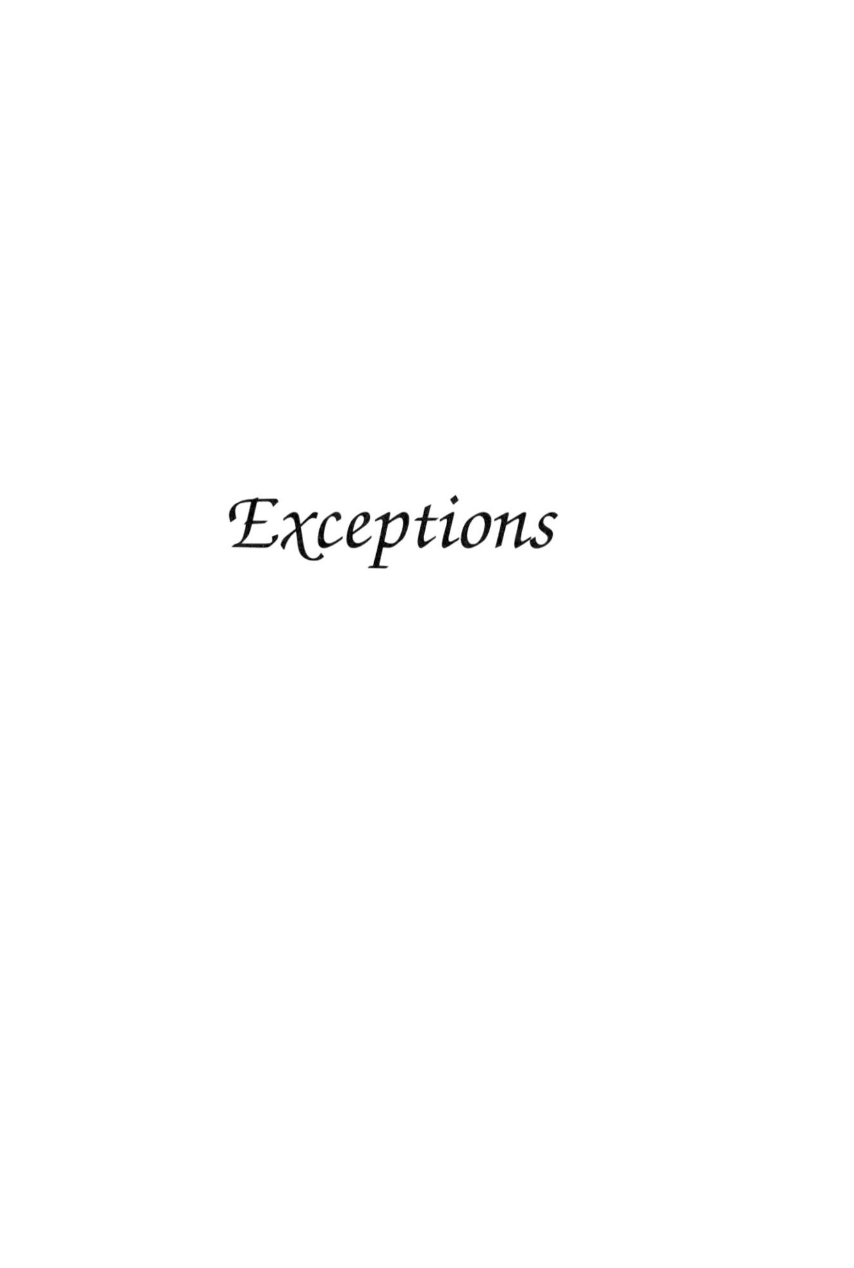

Exceptions

One Last Souvenir

As a couple we're quite a success!
We've had a very fine marriage, my dear.
And I wouldn't have settled for less;
Just being your wife was the perfect career.

We've had a very fine marriage, my dear;
The best anyone could possess.
Just being your wife was the perfect career;
Love flourished in joy and distress.

The best anyone could possess,
Though our budget, at times, was austere.
Love flourished in joy and distress,
And I'm writing one last souvenir.

Though our budget, at times, was austere,
We are nearing life's ending, I guess.
And I'm writing one last souvenir
Through the tear drops I cannot suppress.

We are nearing life's ending, I guess.
May this token of love make it clear,
Through the tear drops I cannot suppress,
That I've treasured each wonderful year.

And I wouldn't have settled for less.
May this token of love make it clear—
As a couple we're quite a success,
We've had a very fine marriage, my dear!

Ode to Buffoons Everywhere

Do you suppose when comics die
They play "The Palace in the Sky?"
Do audiences there applaud
Pratfalls, quips and antics broad?

Is Heaven wide enough and big
To land each one of them a "gig?"
Will Jessel, Berle, or Benny steal
A clever fellow comic's spiel?

Shall proper matrons look askance
If Hope or Skelton drops his pants?
And will Durante, with panache,
Find his "Mrs. Calabash?"

Perhaps when it's their time to go,
They'll shuffle off *from* Buffalo?
Each one of them, in youth or age,
Must "die" — but (God forbid <u>on</u> <u>stage</u>?)

Since I'm a fan who loves to laugh,
Please grant this boon on my behalf:
Beloved clowns, if we should meet,
Reserve for me a front row seat.

Blankety-Blank Verse

I'll never know why poets use
That unrhymed form of verse.
They call it "blank" (and I agree!)
But free style's even worse.

To learn the reason I'll attempt
To write this poem *sans* rhyme.
Here goes: it won't be easy, but
I'll get it done some(~~time~~) DAY.

Oops! I'll try again because I know
That *I* control this pen!
Perhaps I'll write romantic thoughts
Of women and their (~~men~~) MATES.

Now this is just ridiculous;
But one last try I'll make.
No use! And what is more, I've got
An awful stomach (~~ache~~) PAIN.

Uh–oh — the pain is lower down;
I'm hoping it will pass.
I wonder if I've placed it wrong
And the pain is in my (A—) TUSH!

It just won't work — I must concede
It's harder than I'd planned.
But since they do what I cannot,
I'll give them all a "hand!"

Limericks

I

A short-tempered mobster from Kent
On his "Caddy" discovered a dent.
His girl friend confessed,
Now she's quite statuesque
In an outfit of Portland cement.

II

A dumb nurse was asked to explain
The medical term "labor pain."
She replied, "By and large
It means someone in charge,
About whom the unions complain."

III

A Texas-type cowboy from Queens
Was asked to define "Haute Cuisines."
"These are tacos," he said,
"Which are tastefully spread
On a bed of de-gassed refried beans."

IV

A sailor (and Chauvinist pig!)
Had an ego uncommonly big.
But he dug his own grave
When he fondled a WAVE—
Now he's doing two years in the brig.

V

A shyster accustomed to sleaze
Charged his clients exhorbitant fees.
He'd say with a grin
"Now before we begin,
My retainer will cost you ten G's."

VI

A delinquent young "jock" prone to tricks,
When accused of slam-dunking three bricks
Through a school window pane,
Countered, " *You* should complain?—
I was shooting for five out of six!"

Little Willies

I

Willie robbed a liquor store;
Helped himself to booze galore.
Mother frowned, "Will, don't you think
You're really much too young to drink?"

II

Willie, in a playful mood,
Went to school completely nude.
Mother said when class recessed,
"At least he wasn't over-dressed."

III

Willie with a baseball bat
Clubbed to death an alley cat.
Mother made a gagging noise;
Father said, "Boys *will* be boys."

IV

Will stabbed father with a fork;
Father's buried in New York.
Mother said, "The true aesthete
Uses knives, not forks on meat."

V

Willie set a church on fire,
Watching priests and nuns expire.
Mother asked, "On *Sunday* yet?
Where's your sense of etiquette?"

VI

Willie "mooned" a passing car,
Trying to be popular.
Father said, "While fun is fun—
That looks a bit too 'cheeky,' son."

Bee-havior

When earth was new, the female bee
Kept busy hatching progeny.
Appalled by bees' first census poll,
God gave her pills for birth control.

But busy breeding, never still—
She soon forgot to take the pill.
And that is why in times like these,
There are so many sons of bees!

To An Editor

To one who can murder my brainchild
With a stab of your blue-pencil "knife:"
Refrain please from zealous excesses
In taking so precious a life.

If surgery must be conceded,
Then cut! But take care with your wrist.
An occasional slash may be needed—
But must it be done with a twist?

Aloha McAllen

A rusty old tow-car with trailer in back
Substitutes fine for "my little grass shack."
The friendly folks here I find much the same
As those smiling Hawaiians of Waikiki fame.
The trees and plants here very nicely compare
To the similar palms and the greenery there.
We also have music and birdsong, you know,
Just as they do where the pineapples grow.
Hawaii is far, but my Valley is near—
And contentment is mine every day of the year.

Aloha Oi Weh!

I was born in Honolulu,
Though conceived in Tel Aviv.
Mine father's name is Abie
And mine Mama's Esther Eve.

I teach the tourists hula
In Oahu's best resorts,
And I mostly date kanakas
'Cause they look so cute in shorts.

But I also dance the hora;
I like bagels with my poi,
And I learned (in perfect Yiddish)
How to sing "Aloha Oe."

Mine parents call me Sadie—
But according to the courts,
Mine legal name is really
Tondeleyo Sadie Schwartz.

Bread And Gravy

We had two sons, one named Davey
Who hated meat—loved bread and gravy.
And I was just his cook and slavey
Until he left to join the Navy.

The Navy told him what to eat:
Salads, soups, and (horrors!) *meat*,
To win him from the bread and gravy.
Of course they failed, just like his slavey.

When Dave rebelled, they shaved his head
With curses better left unsaid.
They served him water with his bread,
But not a single tot of gravy.

Then Davey tried a week-long fast;
Got hauled before a Captain's Mast.
He won! They sent him home at last—
And guess who serves him bread and gravy?

Now I'm the one who just can't win;
My hair is staighter than a pin.
But Davey's hair has grown back in
And (just my luck) *his* grew in wavy!

Today Dave swaggers like a king;
Spends little time in listening.
He credits his curls and everything
To all that (bleeping!) bread and gravy.

by N.E.C. (The Royal Slavey)

Catastrophe

The lady's name is Tiger
And she's got a jealous streak;
Ignore her for a moment
And she's angry for a week.

She stays out half the night
(While doing God knows *what!*)
The neighbors told me months ago
She nothing but a slut.

Fidelity is not her style;
I'll spare you the details,
But her offspring all were sired by
A dozen different males.

I cannot use the phone in peace;
For if I talk too long—
She'll bite me on the ankle
Just to teach me right from wrong.

Ann-Margaret thought that title hers,
Of "Kitten with a whip."
She lost it to a cat that purrs
While giving me a nip.

I bought her once a catnip toy;
(The field mice brought a bell).
But oh, she fills my life with joy—
That Tiger-Cat from Hell!

Fractured Mother Goose

I

Hey Diddle Diddle—
A "cat" with a fiddle
Was playing out of tune.
The audience laughed
As the customers quaffed
And the crowds overflowed the saloon!

II

Mary, Mary, quite contrary:
How can your garden grow
With dreck (like bells
And cockle shells)
And herds of Buffalo?

III

Jack and Jill,
Who climbed that hill
To get a drink of water,
Are on the run;
Her pappy's gun
Jammed — or he'd have shot her!

Perceptions

Perceptions

I have listened dismayed to distorted abuse
From the self-styled "religiously right."
Too often I've heard their Neanderthal views
Expounded in venomous spite.
Now I'm tuning them out, having listened too long
To the hopelessly-biased "religiously wrong!"

Gothic Haiku

I

The crocus comes to life
In Spring,
Ridiculing Winter's sting.

II

The rose enhances
Summer's haze.
Fragrance permeates
My days.

III

Chrysanthemums pay
Autumn's rent—
Golden coinage, wisely spent.

IV

The winter asters
Linger last,
Holding hearts in
Pleasure fast.

Music In A Villanelle

There's music in a villanelle
As charming as a symphony
That makes my soul with rapture swell.

It beckons as a carrousel,
An ariose calliope—
There's music in a villanelle.

And frequently it may dispel
Bleak moods into a rhapsody
That makes my soul with rapture swell.

Then I am held within the spell
Of poignant, flowing melody.
There's music in a villanelle.

Its lilting cadences compel
A song of lyric poetry
That makes my soul with rapture swell.

It thrills me as a mission bell
That tolls the coming Jubilee.
There's music in a villanelle
That makes my soul with rapture swell!

Echo's Response

Life posed many questions which left me perplexed.
I longed for a husband; so what I did next
Was to visit the mountains where Echo holds sway,
To learn what advice about men she'd convey.
I shouted my queries to Echo, and when
Her answers resounded — I learned about men!

I asked:

"Think you all men are troublesome?"
Echo candidly said, "Some."

"What lies behind man's plunderage?"
Echo's sad reply was "Rage!"

"What lacks who deems himself first class?"
Echo sharply muttered, "Class."

"Which lack most merits *your* distaste?"
Echo's prompt reply was "Taste."

"When wed, shall I his misdeeds know?"
The nymph, with laughter, shouted "No!"

"But must I my own faults confess?"
At this, she ruefully sighed, "Yes."

"And what redeems *him* from disgrace?"
Echo softly whispered, "Grace."

"What then shall be his masterpiece?"
The final sound I heard was — "Peace."

To A Mirror

These lines and wrinkles are a sham,
They cannot speak of who I am,
Nor blemish of an aging skin
Betray the girl who dwells within.

Though cheek may droop and chin may sag,
The child inside still waves the flag
And quick-steps to the lilting tunes
Of dancing clowns and gay buffoons!

How sad that those who worship "youth"
Can never comprehend this truth.
O mirror, you reflect a lie—
For I am young until I die!

For Robin – Our First Grandchild

When Robin beckons me to play
She somehow seems to be
Unmindful that my hair is gray,
And I am over three.

Despite attempts to mold her,
A miracle has sprung;
For she keeps growing older
While I am growing young!

Joy To <u>Our</u> World

We celebrated Christmas;
Went caroling this year.
(They needed help at nursing homes—
Too tired to volunteer).

We baked our Christmas turkey;
Then gobbled up the feast.
(They called for folks to serve the poor—
We sent our parish priest).

We spent the whole week shopping
And bought ourselves a gift.
(We meant to visit orphan kids—
But time flew by too swift).

We decked our halls with holly
Had brunch at the Savoy.
(I hope God saw how hard we worked
Dispensing Christmas joy)!

Comments for Poet Markham

He drew a circle that shut me out,
Heretic, rebel — a thing to flout.
But Love and I had the wit to win —
We drew a circle that took him in.
Edwin A. Markham

O heretic rebel whom "he" circled out:
I credit your love — it's your wit that I doubt.
Far better to picket the country club gate
For the Blacks and the Jews, and all victims of hate.

For a love that exclusively helps only *one*
Is easily flouted and benefits none.
Your intentions are good and our aims are akin,
But changing the "system" is where to begin!

It's Never Too Late

There's one thing that aging can't alter,
(For thanks to God's marvelous plan)
Mere decades won't cause us to falter—
We can if we think that we can.

Let each so-called "oldster" remember
That youth was when troubles began,
And Maytime can't rival December—
We can if we think that we can.

Find hobbies and interests in living,
Don't sit on your lonely divan.
Real friendships are founded on giving—
You can if you think that you can.

At bedtime when doubts may come creeping,
Just snuggle up close to your man;
And tell him to knock off the weeping—
He can if he thinks that he can!

Literacy vs. Lunacy

The art of conversing has withered away
From the use and abuse of the well-worn cliche.
Examples: "What's cookin?" and "Whaddayasay?"

Good manners that everyone used to applaud
Give way to rude comments (so dear to the clod).
Example: "Gettaloada da jugs on dat broad!"

Grand opera and concerts may disappear soon.
Bad taste is contagious and none seem immune.
Examples: punk rock or a hill-billy tune.

Lest all these Neanderthal creatures compel
Our surrender of culture and pleasure as well—
Let's buy them all 'one-way excursions' to Hell.

Song Of A Spinster

My married friends ask why I've never been wed,
Or needed a husband for warming my bed.
A jail cell is warm, but its tenant's not free—
O the celibate life style is perfect for me!

My relatives wonder why I've never wed,
Or needed a husband for earning my bread.
The answer is this: I prefer to live free—
O the celibate life style is perfect for me!

My spinster friends say I've been sadly misled
And that someday I'll rue never having been wed.
My rejoinder is "Nonsense!" and "Fiddle-de-dee!"
O the celibate life style is perfect for me!

I've firmly decided I never shall wed,
Or ever shell out for a match-maker's fee.
I intend to keep "playing the field" though, instead—
As this celibate life style is perfect for me!

Beacons Of Hope

*(Written at the time of the National Mother's
March for Polio Research)*

This evening let each porch light glow
Reflecting friendly warmth within,
And welcome with a glad "Hello"
Each marching-mother heroine.

For mothers march that children may,
As children should, be free from pain.
They march so crippled legs today,
Tomorrow will be strong again.

So let your lighted beacons shine
As long ago His star once shone.
Remember — but for Grace Divine,
The child they help could be your own.

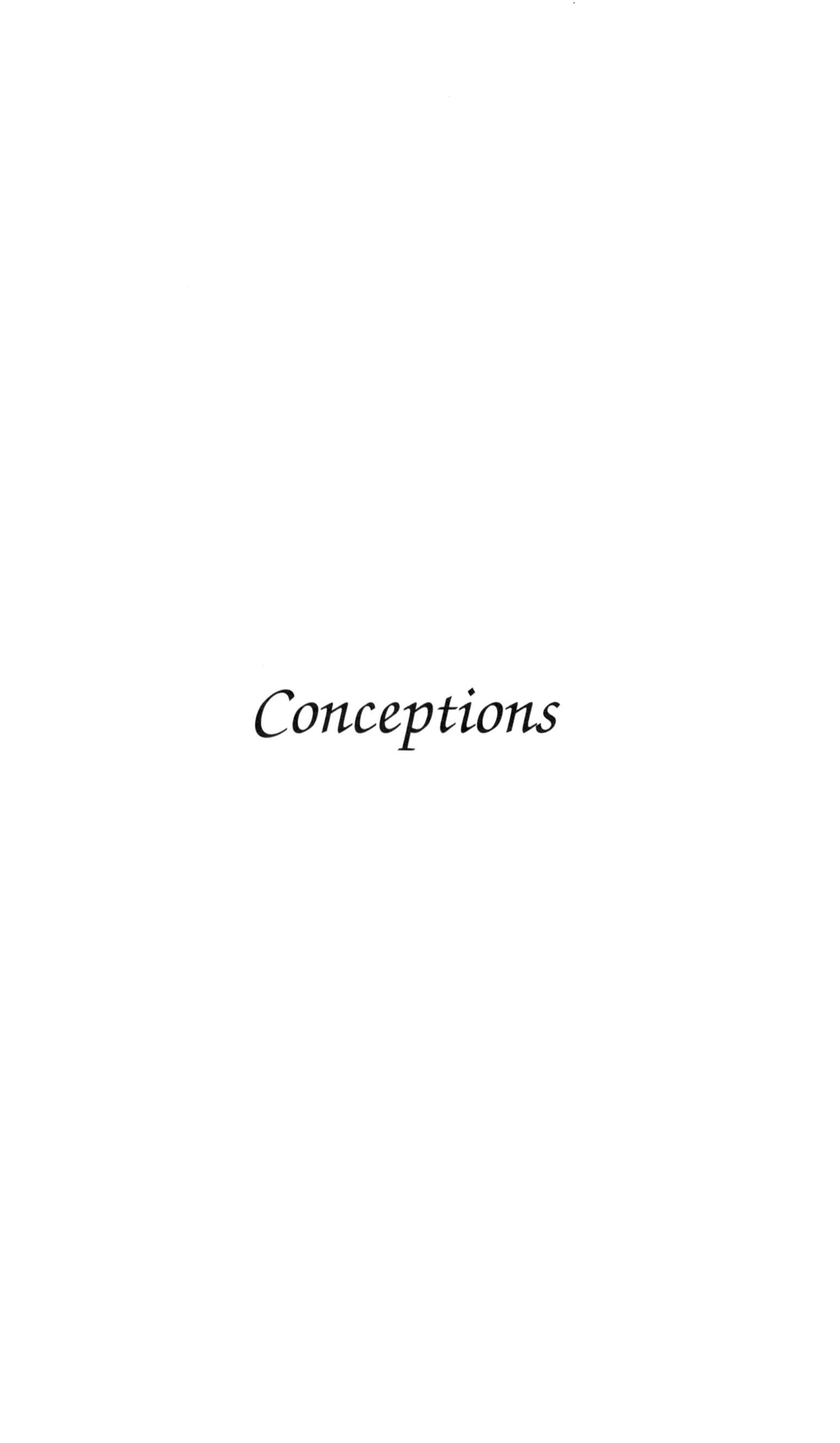

Conceptions

Conceptions

A poem resembles man's cycle of birth,
As each tender seedling takes start
From fertile ideas expanding in worth
When nourishment flows from the heart;
And the Muse leaves the poet exhausted and worn
From the labor of love men call art.
But joy fills the earth when an infant is torn
From creation's full womb every glorious morn
That a baby arrives — or a poem is born!

To A Great-Grandchild

Although two generations divide us,
When I gazed on your newness I smiled.
Then I prayed that the world would treat gently
The child of the child of my child.

Credo

I think that unicorns exist
With horn of pearl and amethyst.
I know that Camelot is there
Amidst my castles in the air.

And I am sure that angels dance
With joy at man's deliverance.
Forgive me if I find it odd
That some cannot believe in *God!*

The Prison

(A Prologue)

Hades, in contrast to all I've been told,
I sense is a dungeon of merciless cold;
And those who inhabit each bone-chilling cell
Must long for the mythical fires of Hell!
Their souls lie encased, not in flame but in frost,
While mine shares despair with the frozen ones lost.
Reliving the glow of a golden sun's rays,
Of oven-warm kitchens and hot summer days,
I wonder if Heaven-sent heat from above
Will thaw my cold spirit and fill it with love.

Jail Break

(The Epilogue)

The cold prison bars are now melting away—
I scheduled a breakout for half-past today;
And all that impeded escape from that cell
Were the icy-cold bars enclosing my Hell.
The shackles, long-formed by a demon inside,
Were merely the fetters of anger and pride.
The jailer I dreaded (yet never could see)
I found in a mirror was no one but me.
The exit was easy — I walked out the gate
Free from the burdens of envy and hate.

The Sinners Three

It's difficult to grasp the scope
Of evil in the misanthrope
Who robs his fellow man of hope.

And harder still to long esteem
The mischief maker who would scheme
To steal away another's dream.

But the sorriest of mankind's throng
Commits an even greater wrong—
To take from any man his song!

This Child

This child, albeit woman grown,
Was living in apostasy;
And drifting unaware, alone
Upon a vast uncharted sea.
This child, who often disobeyed
Thy given precepts carelessly,
Knew little of the ransom paid
Upon that cross at Calvary.

This child, remorseful, sought in vain
Through prayer to reunite with Thee,
Hoping somehow she might gain
Forgiveness in Thy clemency.

This child, whose spirits upward soared
When Thou received her thankfully,
Heard "*Love* thy neighbor" (blessed Word!)
"And know that thou art loved by me."

Visions And Dreams

The Heaven my fanciful visions perceive
Encourages learning, so that souls may receive
What only a genius on earth could achieve.

Great portals of pearl stand wide open to all;
And welcoming signs adorning each wall
Reassure new arrivals awaiting His call.

The streets, some of gold and still others of clay,
Lead bankers and paupers alike on their way
To the mansions (or hovels) where either might stay.

The biblical warnings of penalties steep
Were told in the words "As ye sow, shall ye reap."
But the faithful of God who have tended His sheep
Shall be wakened by angels from death's final sleep.

The Answer

To overcome this sorry world,
We first must quell the Beast
That dwells within our tortured souls
Till all men are deceased.
The Armageddon with ourselves,
This struggle must be won,
Or lost shall be the greater war
With victory for none.
Salvation comes through Christ alone;
On Him we must depend
As signs of final days appear
Foretelling mankind's end.
We need not overcome the world;
Our problems lie within.
But when we learn to trust the Lord
And turn away from sin,
The Gospel promise will come true—
To conquer death and win.

I Can

When doubting one's own talents
And self-confidence seems small,
We must restore the balance
To be lifted lest we fall.
But knowing well in Whom to trust,
We fear no mortal man.
When Jesus says, "My child, you must–"
The answer is "I can!"

A Tale of Twin Cities

(Niagara Falls, New York and Niagara Falls, Ontario)

Both share the majestical waterfalls,
As high as the river runs deep.
Niagara, in thundering rapture calls,
Flowing on while the twin cities sleep.

All five of the Iroquois nations there thrived,
Planting bounteous harvests in peace.
Their tribal lore, customs and stories survived
About monster-fish, roebuck and geese.

And the saga of fair Lelawala's brave ride
(Their maid of the legends and mist);
How the River-God chose her to come be his bride—
How she perished in keeping their tryst!

How white men came later and with them the wars,
As the history books all can attest.
So Hail to Niagara, the pride of the East
And our world renowned gate to the West!

Forgiveness

Forgiveness, though a state very hard to attain,
Was created alike for the pure and profane.
It's a thing that, when granted, can render one whole,
Yet a thing, when denied, that can sever one's soul!
It's a thing to be shared so a grievance can mend
And the enemy lost be replaced by a friend.

Deceptions

Deceptions

1390 A.D.

Rumplestiltskin was my name—
Stealing babies was my game.
I harmed no child, yet history's wrath
Has labelled me a "psychopath!"

1990 A.D.

Jeffrey Dahmer is my name—
Killing children was my game.
Because I found they taste delicious,
The prosecution called me "vicious!"

In ages past, none got off free;
Today most felons cop a plea.
In measurements of guilt, it's strange
How attitudes and values change.

The Candidate

His eyes, wide open to the dreams of power,
(Will they be blinded to the public weal?)
His promises, created for the hour,
(Will they survive the graft and crooked deal?)
His conscience now concerned for public duty,
(Will it ignore that call for private gain?)
His memory, recalling truth and beauty,
(Will it remember *after* the campaign?)
His ears, attuned to all and all conceding,
(Will they become enamored of his voice?)
This winsome creature we elect, unheeding,
(How long will he *remain* the people's choice?)

Ode (Owed?) To A Used Car Salesmen

Though aware of the truth in the saying
"What glitters is not always gold,"
We still believe hucksters conveying
That only 'real bargains' are sold;
Just to learn, after rueful assaying,
How rarely 'real bargains' are bought.
And to find, past semantical playing,
How seldom real liars are caught!

The 'Virgin' Mary

I decided to make my guests cocktails;
Bloody-Marys (*sans* vodka) I chose.
I'd cooked them a fabulous dinner,
With cocktails for the toasts I'd propose.

They knew that I can't abide liquor,
And this cocktail attempt was my first;
Yet I hoped they'd enjoy my endeavor—
But what followed was really the worst.

The Honored-guest sipped, then he shuddered.
"What's this garbage!" I heard him exclaim.
"I call that a real Bloody-Mary," I said;
But he called it "a real bloody shame!"

Mea Culpa

(Commemorating the start of Diet #573)

When I lose my control and go off on a binge,
All my friends are too quick to condemn;
For my conscience eventually gives me a twinge—
Who am I kidding? Not them.

When I snack in midmorning or midafternoon,
(Or even awaiting a bus)
And I swear it's a habit I'll break very soon—
Who am I kidding? Not us.

When late in the evening sheer boredom sets in
And I reach for a cookie or two,
While telling myself that one day I'll be thin—
Who am I kidding? Not you.

When I use no-cal syrup on hotcakes galore,
Thus making them calorie free,
I am helping my diet as gaily I pour—
Who am I kidding? Just me!

Illusions

They strip off their clothes for a living,
Flaunting their bodies with ease.
Dancing nude, *sans* a single misgiving,
They tantalize, posture and tease.

Yet they hide every innermost feeling
As they play out their make-believe roles.
I wonder what hurts they're concealing,
Locked deep in their piteous souls.

Cory Richard

(A parody of the poem "Richard Cory"
by Edward A. Robinson)

Whenever Cory Richard came to town,
We citizens *en masse* looked down on him.
He was a vagabond, a ragged clown,
Unshaven and of visage rather grim.

And he was always sloppily arrayed,
And he was always cursing when he talked.
The clothes he wore were generally frayed,
And he would sometimes stumble as he walked.

And he was poor — yes, poor as anything
And lacking both in manners and in grace.
In short, we thought that he was everything
To make us glad that we weren't in his place.

So on we smirked and gloated till the night
Policemen found poor Cory Richard dead.
They searched his shack to find upon the site
One million dollars hidden in his bed!

The Foolish Virgin

I once wrote a poem, long-crumbled to dust
On my virginal oak chiffonier.
It told my young, fanciful stirrings of lust
For that dream man who'd one day appear.

I later composed wistful songs in the rain,
While I yearned for one, handsome and tall.
Years passed while I hoped, but awaited in vain
An Adonis to answer my call.

Then just when I felt quite abandoned by Fate,
A plain, loving man heard my cry.
But I liked not his looks, so I fastened the gate—
And a lifetime of love passed me by.

RX For Eternal Youth

A state of youth in permanence
Is merely wishful thought;
And concepts void of common sense
Most always come to naught.

If you would thwart advancing age,
Leave vanity behind.
Quit using wrinkles as your gauge—
Instead explore the mind!

These blemishes which often strike
Are only folds of skin.
Intelligence attracts its like,
And lasts through thick and thin.

Sonnet To Humor

(Mine — not Longfellow's)

I shot an arrow in the air
That might have landed anywhere,
Except I took especial care
To hit our neighbor's derriere.

Though targets such as this are rare,
My aim was true — I hit it square.
It really gave him quite a scare;
You should have heard the fellow swear!

Then father, with an angry glare,
Reached out and grabbed me by the hair;
Then soundly spanked my bottom bare.
(I guess the punishment was fair.)

And now I'm very careful where
I shoot my arrows in the air!

Thoughts On Going Home

Old times, like fallen drops of rain,
Can ne'er be gathered up again;
And friends we used to entertain
Become just blurs in memory.

Others now and then complain
How time and distances constrain;
But people change and few remain
Unaltered in their constancy.

Old haunts that once were our domain
Have disappeared! We seek in vain,
Past city street and country lane,
For relics of antiquity.

Honest folks must surely see
(Although some few might disagree)
The simple truth shall ever be—
We never can go home again!

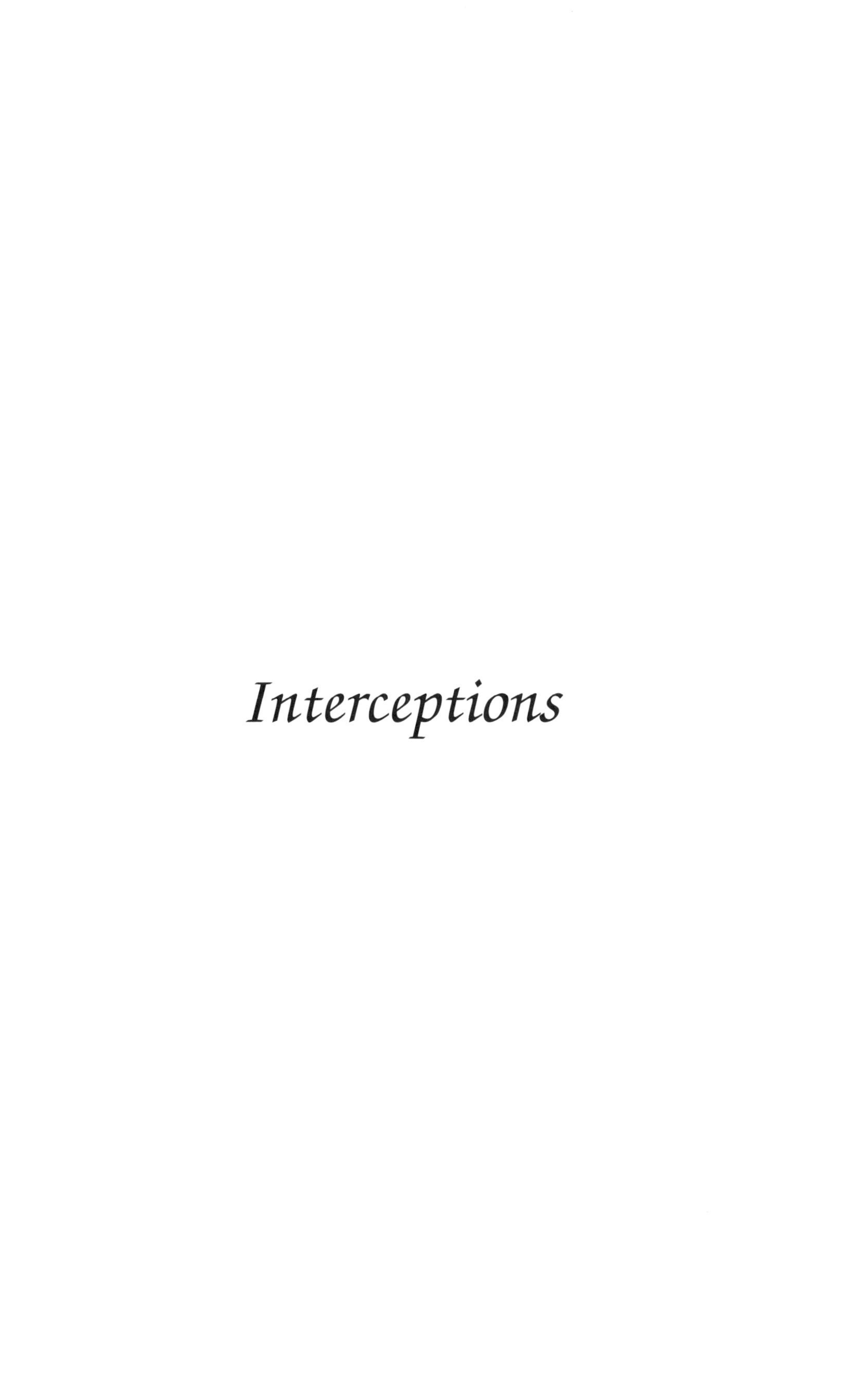

Interceptions

Lamentation

I am but held in sorrow fast—
The child has died that in me grew!
They say that weeping cannot last
And life shall once again renew.

This grief will pass (say those who know),
Indeed, my tears no longer drop.
But where did all the colors go?
And when did all the music stop?

Of My Son

I weep, but as the hours pass
I think of all the lives he touched.
His own, though short, was full — and then
I hear him softly say "Amen."

**by Glenn Church – husband of the
author and father of William S. Church**

Lullaby For My Mother

*(Dedicated to the memory of Myrtle B. Brenner,
mother of the author)*

You cradled me softly when I was new-born.
And yet, so it seems at your grave as I mourn,
That we have changed places (in fantasy wild)
And I seem the mother, with you as my child.
Now sleep in the arms of our Father above—
May mother and child find repose in His love!

Requiem For A Daughter

(Written to honor the memory of
Donna Jeanne Rurey-Iselin)

When you, beloved daughter, left
To live in God's eternal fold,
And we, so suddenly bereft
Were comfortless and all acold—
We sought release from sorrow's chain
In prayer, but said "Thy will be done!"
Then He, Who understood our pain,
Who once had mourned a martyred Son,
Flung open Heaven's vast domain
To welcome home our precious one.

In Tribute

(Dedicated to the memory of the late Everett Dobson)

Our world today seems less than whole,
For it has lost a noble soul
Whose quiet ways and gentle mind
Bespoke the best in humankind.
May Heaven's angels now attend
A valued and beloved friend.

In Memoriam

(Of the late fire Captain, Edward Barszcz)

I count myself as one of those bereft,
Since death has taken friend, as well as man;
And ask myself, "Can naught of him be left?
Must friendship end with life's brief, measured span?"

Then understanding comes and I rejoice,
Convinced we'll meet again in just a while.
I still can tune my heart to hear his voice;
I still can close my eyes and see his smile.

To memory I'll leave the sad good-byes.
In friendship there is nothing to forgive.
As I confess this truth, my spirits rise
And I am ready, once again, to live.

Legacy Of A Handyman

He told me when to change the oil
And where he kept the mileage chart,
And when the hedges should be trimmed
And how to take a lamp apart.

He showed me how the furnace works
And tricks to make the mower start.
He taught me how to fix all things—
Save how to mend a broken heart!

Do I Miss You?

When you folks moved out West
I was very depressed,
So I phoned every week and I wrote.
But I finally broke free,
Now you're nothing to me—
But a couple of lumps in the throat!

Sonnet To Liberty

The earth-bound man, condemned to snail-like pace,
Holds forth upon the joys of liberty.
He tediously plods from place to place
While watching flocks of sparrows flying free!

The destiny of babies born with "AIDS"
Is constant pain, attached to strange machines.
Their liberty was lost in sorry trades
That only death, in mercy, contravenes.

We all must pay, no matter what the price,
That liberty for everyone prevail.
The choice is ours: to either sacrifice
Or run an ad "America For Sale!"

May Lady Liberty forever stand
And with her torch illuminate our land.

The Golfer's Prayer

If there's one virtue I can claim—
It's this, O Lord, I love the game!
And I would choose, if Thou agree,
To golf throughout eternity.

But there is much that I would know.
Please tell me, Lord, if it be so:
For instance, are the links up there
Given Thy eternal care?

Are Heaven's fairways half so green
As earth's — or merely opaline?
I wonder if I'll qualify,
Or are the entrance fees too high?

And are there Pros in Paradise
To teach me to correct that slice?
Do cherubs drive from star to star,
And do they ever shoot a par?

Pray, do Thy angels weep a lot
When we poor mortals dub a shot?
Before my earth-bound play is done
Will I have scored a hole-in-one?

I know not, Lord, from day to day,
How many rounds that I might play;
But this is all I'm hoping for—
That Thou approve my final score.

On A Golden Wedding Anniversary

Too little time is fifty years
To hold a lifetime's joys and tears.
So quickly carefree youth elapsed,
We hardly noticed when it passed.

One day our souls shall elevate;
And when we meet at Heaven's gate,
I pray the God we both adore
Will grant us fifty eons more.

A Little Grace

We come to Thee in gratitude
To thank Thee once again
For food, for home, for family—
And love unspared. Amen!

A Larger Grace

My "Little Grace" though limited,
Still serves to bless my daily bread.
I deemed it once a paltry phrase,
Inadequate my Lord to praise.

Instead with elegance and flair,
I'd pen a more impressive prayer.
It soon became quite manifest
That "large" does not equate with "best."

God spoke these words in mild reproof:
"Thy longer prayer is too aloof;
I liked its little counterpart
Because it came from out the heart!"